HOUSEKEEPER'S DAUGHTER

By Donald Henderson Clarke

Author of Millie, Impatient Virgin, etc.

●

You'll like this gay and full-blooded tale of the city coun-part of the farmer's daughter who gets more than her share of Greenwich Village love. You may find it a bit frank, but it's all in such good humor that you can hardly object to Mr. Clarke's easy handling of the so-called "facts of life."

From the moment the Rev. Paul F. Maxon rents his house in Greenwich Village to J. Robert Randall, a reporter on the New York Planet, things begin to happen. Robert says he wants a place to write a thesis, but he has also looked upon the luscious curves of Hilda Kreemhild, daughter of the Rev. Maxon's housekeeper.

Of the pursuit of Hilda, of Benny, the melancholy murderer, of high thoughts and low impulses, of drinking, of drought and devastation (the latter wrought by Hilda's Beauty), of the unspeakable but lovable Deacon and his autumnal love affair, of Margaret Havey, who went unkissed until forty but who could not resist the Deacon's wooing, of Manny and Okey-Doke (even lower in the social scale than reporters), of Olga and of her husband, whose ignorance of the Mendelian Law all but wrecked their marriage — of these and of many other matters Mr. Clarke tells us, and at the end the reader, pop-eyed with excitement and exhausted with laughter, can only murmur: "A mad world, my masters."

Now Only $1.98

●

SUPER MAIL ORDER DEPT.
137 Wellington St. West — Toronto, Ontario

Nippy

STORIES

JUNE, 1945

NIPPY STORIES is published by SUPER PUBLICATIONS at Suite 801, 137 Wellington St. W., Toronto, Ontario. All contributions should be addressed to that office and the editor stipulates that he will not be responsible for loss or damage of unsolicited contributions, although they will be carefully taken care of. Contents copyright. Printed in Canada. **Twenty-five cents a copy.**

HOT DIGGITY!

"She said your songs took her back to her girl-
hood."

"Yes; my voice carries a good way."

* * *

"After her rich uncle heard her sing, he offered
to send her abroad."

"To cultivate her voice?"

"I don't think so."

* * *

To sing is human; to forgive, divine.

"Would you advise me to cultivate my voice?"

"Sure, cultivate it, and for heaven's sake, bury
it deep."

* * *

"Can you sing the Marseillaise?"

"Sure! Marseillaise in the cold, cold ground."

* * *

"What's the matter with your singing? It doesn't
sound right."

"I'm only hitting on one tonsil."

* * *

"Is that a popular song he is singing?"

"It was before he began singing it."

"He's off a sub and he says this is practically a suite for him."

"Oh, Sergeant, I want you to meet my mother-in-law,
and may the best man win!"

"Do you use a bucket to bail out?"

SHAVETAIL ORIGIN

One of the G.I. tom-tom beaters here recently received word from a pal of his in Chicago which sheds new light on the origin of the term "shavetail," nickname of Army second lieutenants. Originally, it referred to an unbroken mule, according to the Dictionary of American English now in preparation at the University of Chicago. The dictionary says the term originated with the Army and was applied to mules because their tails are smooth down to the tufted tip. It later was used with regard to the second looies because of their alleged stubbornness.

"When you're alone there's nothing like playing solitaire for amusement!"

"Could you hurry up your bird studies Professor? The camouflage corps has just assigned me to another post."

"ARMORED HEIFER"
Is—You Guessed It—Canned Milk

"EGG IN YOUR BEER"
Is Too Much Of A Good Thing

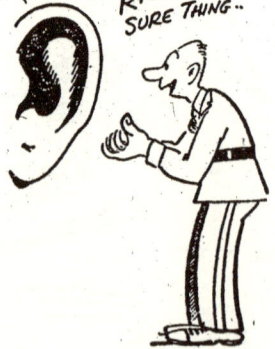

PERILS CONTRASTED

Ffc. Phil Brown, erstwhile Hollywood actor stationed here and attached to the Special Service office, is also a poet whose taste and meter embodies the lyrical gems of Longfellow and Ogden Nash, and perhaps, a smatering of Eddie Guest. To wit:

"If Little Red Riding Hood lived today
  The Modern girl would scorn 'er,
She only had to meet one wolf—
  Not one at every corner!

BUNGSTARTERS FROM OUR OWN LITTLE BEER EMPOURIUM

KLEVER KRAX

Schwankowski, I hear, went into a drug store and bought ten cents worth of asafedia. When he asked the clerk to charge it, the clerk asked him what his name was.

"Schwankowski," he replied.

"Take it for nothing," replied the clerk. "I wouldn't write Schwankowski and asafetida both for ten cents."

*   *   *

"If I leave security equal to what I take away will you trust me till next week?"

"Certainly."

"Well, then, sell me two of these hams and keep one until I return."

*   *   *

"What is a chain store?"

"I suppose it is a place where you buy a marriage license."

"Did I hit it too hard?"

"We won't have a bit of trouble getting a ride as long
as I can keep this tire."

"So sorry Tokio . . . entirely occidental!"

A "FEATHER MERCHANT"
Is A Marine Who Sleeps Too Much.

"GOING UP THE POLE"
Means going on the wagon.

Also An Under-sized Marine who Goes Around saying: "The Bigger They Are, The Harder They Fall"

OLD BUT FAIRLY CLEAN

"What line did you take to Europe last summer?"
"The same line I use around here."

*   *   *

"I called on three kings while I was in Europe."
"How exciting!"
"Worse than that. The other fellow had three aces."

*   *   *

"Where are you from?"
"Saskatchewan."
"What's that, partner?"
"Saskatchewan."
"You no spik Englis'?"

*   *   *

"I know a fellow who was nearly killed by getting up on the wrong side of bed."
"Oh, I'm not superstitious."
"Neither is he, but this was a lower berth."

*   *   *

"Where did you stay in Chicago?"
"I stayed at the Belvedere."
"I stayed at the Belva once, too."

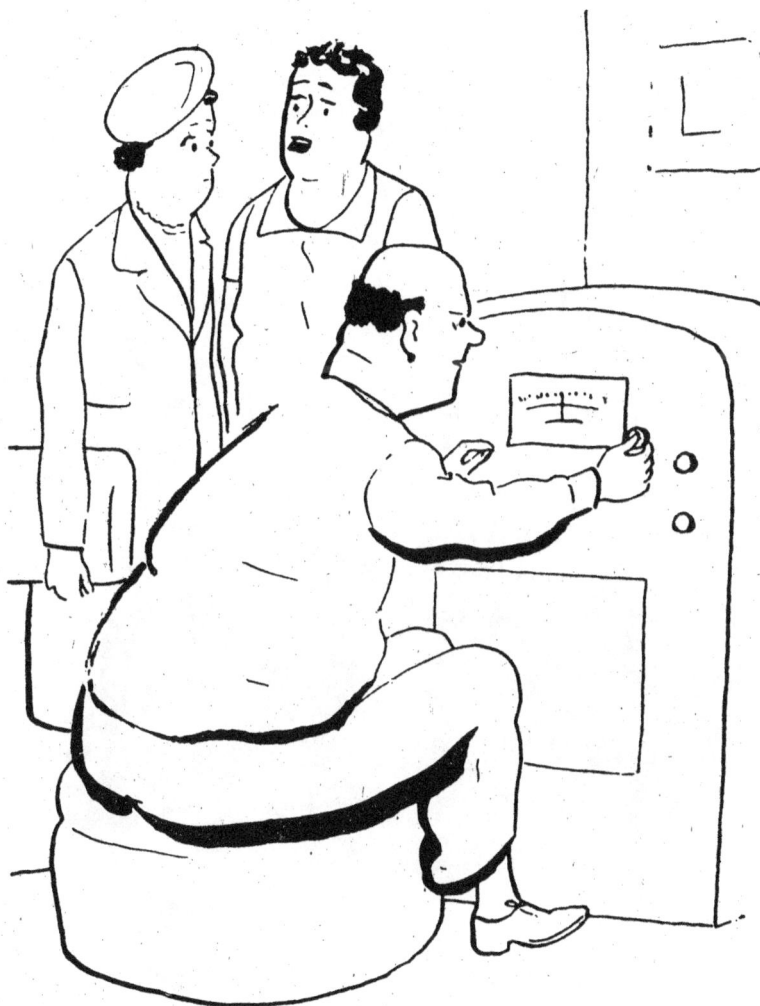

"Once last week George got some music between news broadcasts!"

"Stop comparing me to the Gestapo."

PURE BUNK

This elevator man may not be married, but he's raised a good many families.

* * *

"Her father is familiar with many tongues."
"Ah, a linguist?"
"No, a physician."

* * *

"How is Viola Vacuum getting along in the talking pictures?"
"All right, I guess. She has a double for four-syllable words."

* * *

The farmer gets his living from the soil. So does the washerwoman.

* * *

"What does he do for a living?"
"Paints ob-scenery for a burlesque show."

* * *

"He's an orchestra director—that fellow there."
"That so? He looks to me like a chauffer."
"No. When the musicians get off the train, he'll show them the way to the hotel."

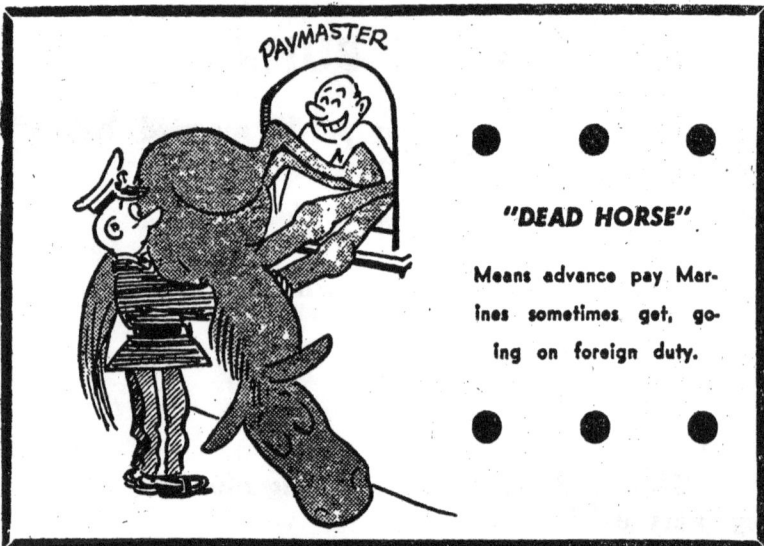

"DEAD HORSE"

Means advance pay Marines sometimes get, going on foreign duty.

"A PLOW-BOY"

Is An Awkward Recruit

"Sa-ay — before I fell asleep I had a chicken tattoed on my chest."

TAKE IT SLOW!

Much had been said and printed about blondes. Much has been said about red-headed women.

* * *

"Why do they call boats 'she'?"
"Because they make a better showing in the wind."

* * *

"Women are puzzles; aren't they?"
"Yes; I had to give up several of them myself."

* * *

"She is the most economical woman I ever met."
"Indeed she is. You'll find she can make one kill last longer than any girl you know."

* * *

"They say women are the salt of the earth."
"Wouldn't doubt it, judging from the number of men they have driven to drink."

* * *

My wife is a wonder woman. She is always wondering where I am.

* * *

The reason so few milkmen are married is that they see so many women early in the morning.

"I met her father. He approves of me."

"Quit wishing for our distress signal to blow away!"

"You're cheating — I dealt you only two aces!"

SNUGGLY SNAGGED

The laugh of the week rightfully belongs on a rookie in Co. C, 79th Inf. Tng. Bn. While making the rounds of the barracks one night last week, a sergeant noticed that one man in particular appeared especially snug in his G. I. rest haven. When asked to arise so the bed could be inspected, the soldier tossed and turned to no avail. He just couldn't get up. A closer inspection revealed that in his haste to retire before taps, he had mistaken the mattress cover for the sheet and had crawled in at the end between the mattress and cover.

* * *

Reporter: "And to what, Mr. Oldtime, do you attribute your longevity?"

Octogenarian: "To the fact, sir, that I never died."

* * *

"I have a wonder watch."

"That watch doesn't look so wonderful to me. How do you mean?"

"Well, it's this way. Every time I look at it, I wonder what time it is."

* * *

I asked him how it was that he was always looking for a job yet never finding it, and he replied, "That's skill, my boy; that's skill."

"Company, Halt!"

"The enemy sees the beer and the sourkraut—he goes to take it, then—*Zippo!*"

'I think I'll feel better when I get Mabel off my chest.'

"We don't like it in there — no one annoyed us!"

"Pardon me, is the seat beneath you taken?"

"He's six feet one inch tall and weighs one hundred eighty five —what caliber do I use?"

"Gee! Thanks for the souvenir, Harry, but I don't think my wife will let me keep her!"

"Well, now, isn't that aggravating?"

"I have here, my friends, one flash photo taken of a couple during the last blackout; what am I bid for it?"

"On the next time around you'd better wake him. He left a 5 o'clock call"

"Well—you wanted me to have evenin' clothes — I spent all my money on them!"

"He does it with a cutout to fool the O.D."

"SOMETHING WENT WRONG, HONEY — THEY DRAFTED. LIZA!"

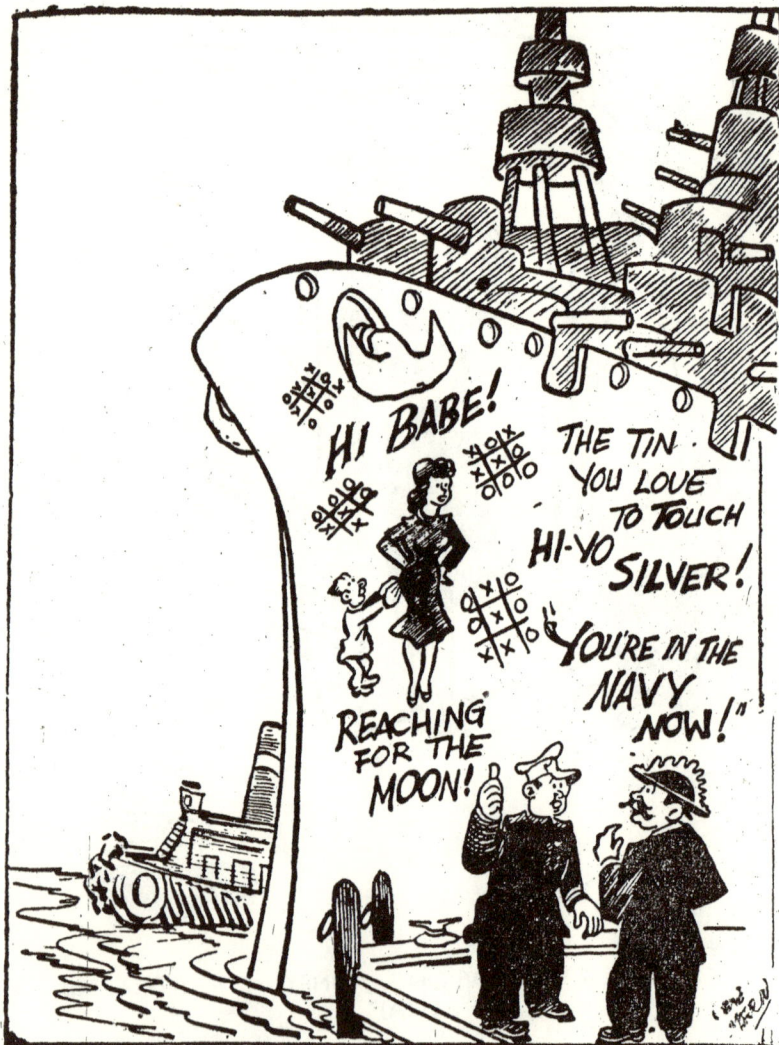

"It's either sabotage or else we have a couple of college boys aboard ship."

"Mother — I have to go out with a sailor like him to give my diary flavor!"

"Major Van Dip — You mean I lose again!"

"WHAT'S COOKIN'

He (over the phone) : "Are you going to be busy this evening?"

She: "No, I'm not!"

H : "Then you won't be tired in th morning; will you?"

*   *   *

"They're applauding something fierce; aren't they?"

"You said something."

*   *   *

"My rival is always taking my part."

"Well, you can't kick about that."

"Yes; I can. I'm an actor"

*   *   *

At the telephone: "Hello."

Answer: "Hello!"

"Hello! Hello!"

Answer: "Hello!"

"My gosh! How this thing echoes!"

*   *   *

She is only a poor telephone girl, but she keeps plugging along.

*   *   *

I don't scoff at miracles any more. I now realize that every time I get the right number on the telephone it is a miracle.

ARTY ANSWERS

"What do you think of this picture?"
"It's a fine picture of a lady. But where's the motor car that ran over her?"

* * *

"I don't think he'll make much ot a success in art."
"Why?"
"He spends too much time drawing corks."

* * *

"Why do you like studies in the nude?"
"I guess it's because I was born that way."

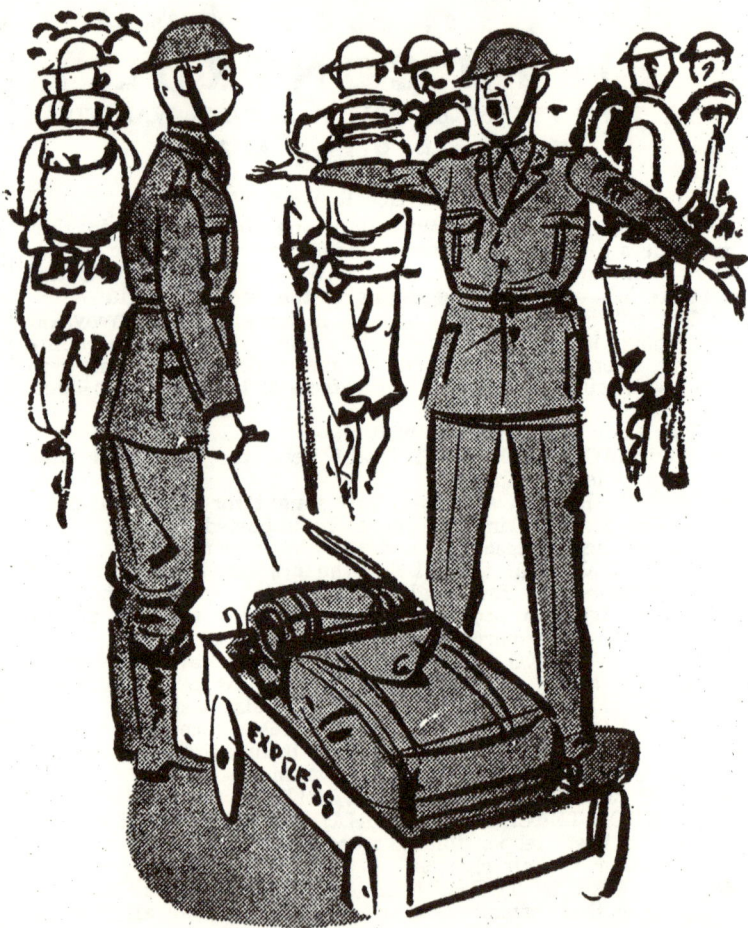

"But, Horace, supposin' you wanted to use wagons?"

"See what I mean—the hand is quicker than the eye!"

"This photo of Jim was taken right after we came out
of that blackout."

NOTICE!
5-HOUR
BLACKOUT
TONITE

"But wait 'till tonight, dearie. It's personality
that counts then."

BACK STAGE

"Have you had any experience in dramatics?"
"Oh, I had my leg in a cast once."

* * *

You can take a chorus girl out of the Follies, but you can't take the follies out of a chorus girl.

* * *

In most Broadway shows, the misses are the hits.

* * *

It's quite a come-down for some people when they are forced to sit in the second balcony. They are used to sitting in the gallery.

* * *

"Most of the stuff exhibited in the circus side shows is barefaced humbug."
"What about the bearded lady?"

* * *

"Don't you think this is a rare bit of art?"
"Yes, 'rare' is the word; it certainly isn't well done."

* * *

Art is long, but a lot of the artists are short.

* * *

"I'm wedded to my art."
"I should think she would divorce you for cruelty."

"Dear, she was only telling me where to get off!"

"Miss me?"

HIGH C!

Some singers get a thousand dollars a night. But look at the risk they run.

* * *

"You know faith will move mountains."

"Yes, I know Mary's faith that she was cut out to be a singer has caused half the neighborhood to move."

* * *

"Have you heard the little Smith girl sing?"
"Yes."
"Don't you think she ought to be sent abroad?"
"Sure. Deport, her by all means."

* * *

"Slim ought to be a good singer."
"Why?"
"He has legs like a canary bird."

* * *

Oh, the man worth while
Is the man who can smile,
While his neighbor struggles along with a song.

* * *

"I am alaways breaking into song."
"If you once get the key, you wouldn't have to break in."

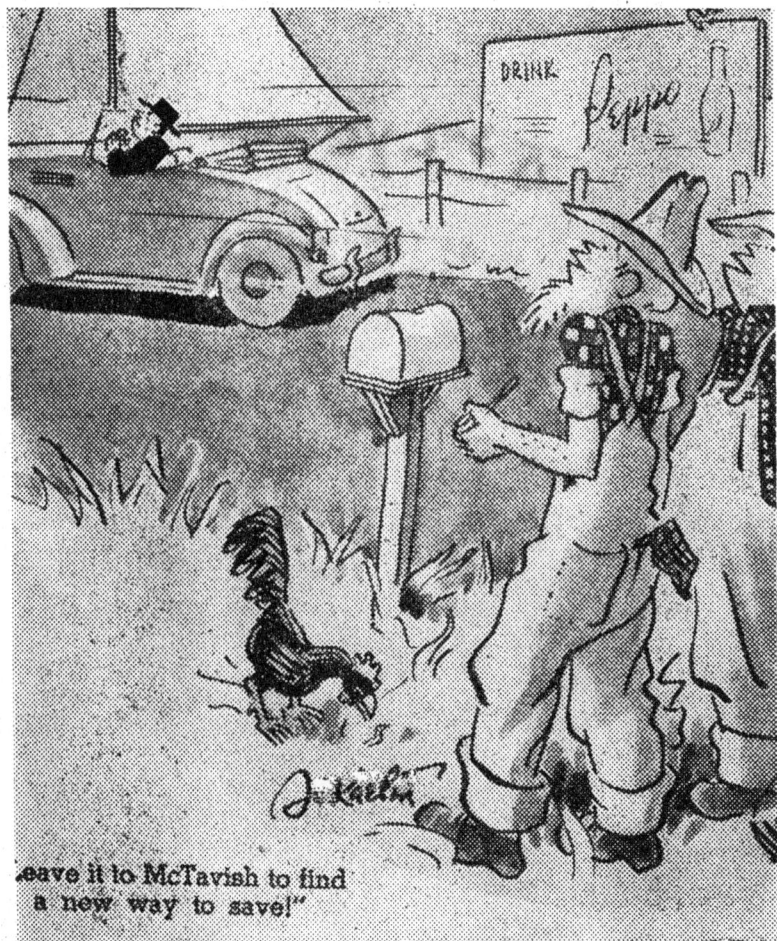

"Leave it to McTavish to find a new way to save!"

"Oh, no floor in particular — we're in no hurry."

"It's been blowing 'em ever since he started washing!"

FROM VERSE TO WORSE

The bugle blows, the day's begun,
And sleepy soldiers are on the run;
Brush your teeth, shine your shoes,
Now they're falling out by two's.

Now they're off to do their work,
Here's a technician and there's a clerk;
Here go the yardbirds out to the field,
To dig up the earth and what it yields.

Some are running, some are talking,
Some are drilling, others squawking;
There's a drill sergeant raising hell,
Because some rookie tripped and fell.

Now don't worry, you'll be led
To victory o'er our enemies' dead.
Eighteen months will fly right by—
Forget your trouble with a shot of rye.

—Sgt. Nissen.
(Aberdeen "Flaming Bomb")

HOW TO MEET MEN AND MARRY

By Juliet Farnham

This book goes far beyond any book published. It is the frankest, most practical book for women ever written. It outlines the secret, feminine technique of how to meet men and marry. It tells you — not in generalities but in specific detail how to meet men even in war time, what to say, what to do and what NOT to do in reaching the most important objective in every woman's life.

In the gay, realistic language of today it tells you step by step how to find the right man for you, how to overcome the obstacles that keep most men from marriage.

The writer has made a deep, searching study of this problem of how to be successful in romance.

Do you find it difficult to meet new men? Do you have trouble in holding the interest of your dates? Do you know just how to turn new acquaintances into a romance? Where to meet men whether you are below average financially, wealthy or in medium circumstances?

You'll find all the answers in this unique, humorous book.

●

SHIPPED POSTPAID

$2.49

●

SUPER MAIL ORDER DEPT.

137 Wellington St. West — Toronto, Ontario

"Aw, Horace, go ahead and do it — he's the colonel's
horse and absolutely thoroughbred."

WISE AND OTHERWISE

I read that the bearded lady of the Great Oompah Circus died recently, leaving a wife and five children.

*   *   *

We notice that the tired business man never gets leg-weary.

*   *   *

"Who is the leading lady in the show?"
"The usher."

*   *   *

"What did you see in the side show?"
"A woman with a man's beard on her face."
"I didn't know they allowed them to neck in public that way."

*   *   *

"This is a charity performance. The actors are all working for nothing."
"Isn't that wonderful? And I think they earn every bit of it, too."

*   *   *

The last show I saw in that town was so rough even the programs were printed on sandpaper.

"I'm not afraid of the wolves — it's the elephants
who bother me!"

DIPSY DOODLES

"My wife can play a saxophone, paint and compose poems."

"Has she any other defects?"

*   *   *

"I bought this picture yesterday."

"I didn't know you were artistic."

"I wasn't. I was drunk."

*   *   *

"Doesn't that picture make you think of Jane?"

"Yes, but I believe Jane uses a little more paint."

*   *   *

"Is he a good artist?"

"Is he? Why, the other day he drew a hen so natural tha when he threw it in the waste basket it laid there."

*   *   *

LATEST PARODY

Officer candidates at North Dakota Agricultural College, the G.I. prep school where enlisted men begin their march — in double time toward a commission, are chanting the popular ditty, "Praise the Lord and Pass the Ammunition," with a slight variation, according to word received by a Camp Roberts rookie:

"Praise the Lord and Pass Me My Commission."

"That makes it three bombers, six pursuit planes, and fourteen sea gulls—how about a duck for supper?"

JUST A BUNK

"I hear you lost your job."

"Oh, not as bad as all that; I found it all right, but when I did, somebody else was working at my desk."

*　　*　　*

"I spent a gruelling half hour."
"Doing what?"

"Feeding the children."

*　　*　　*

"I hear you need a bright, industrious, good-looking young man."

"I do. Whom do you suggest?"

*　　*　　*

I engage only married men. At five o'clock they're not in such a hurry to leave the office.

*　　*　　*

Yes. I am working now. I get good money, but I just don't get enough of it.

*　　*　　*

"What is sadder than a man who loses his last friend?"

"Give it up."

"A man who works for his board and loses his appetite."

"Our electric bill is terrific, so my boy friend suggests blackouts every night!"

"Junior! Have you been into Mama's bubble-bath?"

"Now say—
ahhhhhhhhhhh—!"

"I ran into a door in the blackout—
a bar room door."

"I beg your pardon, somebody pushed me — these crowded phone booths, you know!"

"We'll have to get a new mirror, Dear, this one is beginning to show wrinkles"